50 Italian Pizza Recipes for Home

By: Kelly Johnson

Table of Contents

Classic Margherita Variations:

- Classic Margherita Pizza
- Bufala Margherita
- Prosciutto e Rucola Margherita
- Truffle Oil Margherita

Regional Pizza Styles:

- Neapolitan Pizza
- Roman Pizza (Pizza al Taglio)
- Sicilian Pizza
- Calzone Napoletano
- Focaccia Barese

Seafood Pizzas:

- Pizza Frutti di Mare
- Calamari and Lemon Pizza
- Shrimp Scampi Pizza

Vegetarian Pizzas:

- Rustic Eggplant and Ricotta Pizza
- Mushroom Trifolati Pizza
- Zucchini and Pesto Pizza
- Artichoke and Spinach Pizza

Meat Lover's Pizzas:

- Quattro Carni Pizza
- Spicy Soppressata Pizza
- Bolognese Pizza
- BBQ Chicken Pizza

Gourmet and Unique Pizzas:

- Fig and Prosciutto Pizza
- Smoked Salmon Pizza
- Pumpkin and Sage Pizza
- Caprese Salad Pizza

Dessert Pizzas:

- Nutella and Strawberry Dessert Pizza
- Cannoli Pizza
- Tiramisu Pizza
- Apple Cinnamon Dessert Pizza
- Chocolate and Marshmallow Pizza

Classic Margherita Variations:

Classic Margherita Pizza

Ingredients:

- Pizza dough (store-bought or homemade)
- 1 cup tomato sauce (homemade or good quality store-bought)
- 8 ounces fresh mozzarella, sliced
- Fresh basil leaves
- Extra-virgin olive oil
- Salt and pepper to taste
- Cornmeal or flour for dusting

Instructions:

Preheat the Oven:
- Preheat your oven to the highest temperature it can go, typically around 475-500°F (245-260°C).

Prepare the Dough:
- If using store-bought dough, follow the package instructions for bringing it to room temperature. If making homemade dough, roll it out on a floured surface to your desired thickness.

Prepare the Pizza Peel or Pan:
- If using a pizza stone, sprinkle some cornmeal on a pizza peel. If using a baking sheet, lightly grease it or dust it with flour.

Assemble the Pizza:
- Place the rolled-out dough on the pizza peel or prepared baking sheet.
- Spread the tomato sauce evenly over the dough, leaving a small border around the edges.
- Arrange the fresh mozzarella slices on top of the sauce.
- Season with a pinch of salt and pepper.

Bake the Pizza:
- If using a pizza stone, carefully transfer the pizza to the preheated stone in the oven. If using a baking sheet, simply place it in the oven.
- Bake for about 10-12 minutes or until the crust is golden and the cheese is melted and slightly bubbly.

Finish with Fresh Basil and Olive Oil:
- Once out of the oven, immediately scatter fresh basil leaves over the hot pizza.

- Drizzle extra-virgin olive oil over the top.

Slice and Serve:
- Let the pizza cool for a minute, then slice it into wedges or squares.
- Serve immediately and enjoy the classic Margherita flavor!

Feel free to customize this recipe by adding a sprinkle of Parmesan, a drizzle of balsamic glaze, or a dash of red pepper flakes if you like a bit of heat.

Bufala Margherita

Ingredients:

- Pizza dough (store-bought or homemade)
- 1 cup tomato sauce (homemade or good quality store-bought)
- 8 ounces buffalo mozzarella, sliced
- Fresh basil leaves
- Extra-virgin olive oil
- Salt and pepper to taste
- Cornmeal or flour for dusting

Instructions:

Preheat the Oven:
- Preheat your oven to the highest temperature it can go, typically around 475-500°F (245-260°C).

Prepare the Dough:
- If using store-bought dough, follow the package instructions for bringing it to room temperature. If making homemade dough, roll it out on a floured surface to your desired thickness.

Prepare the Pizza Peel or Pan:
- If using a pizza stone, sprinkle some cornmeal on a pizza peel. If using a baking sheet, lightly grease it or dust it with flour.

Assemble the Pizza:
- Place the rolled-out dough on the pizza peel or prepared baking sheet.
- Spread the tomato sauce evenly over the dough, leaving a small border around the edges.
- Arrange the buffalo mozzarella slices on top of the sauce.
- Season with a pinch of salt and pepper.

Bake the Pizza:
- If using a pizza stone, carefully transfer the pizza to the preheated stone in the oven. If using a baking sheet, simply place it in the oven.
- Bake for about 10-12 minutes or until the crust is golden and the buffalo mozzarella is melted and slightly bubbly.

Finish with Fresh Basil and Olive Oil:
- Once out of the oven, immediately scatter fresh basil leaves over the hot pizza.
- Drizzle extra-virgin olive oil over the top.

Slice and Serve:
- Let the pizza cool for a minute, then slice it into wedges or squares.
- Serve immediately and enjoy the rich and creamy goodness of Bufala Margherita!

Feel free to add a touch of grated Parmesan, a sprinkle of oregano, or a drizzle of balsamic glaze for additional flavor if desired.

Prosciutto e Rucola Margherita

Ingredients:

- Pizza dough (store-bought or homemade)
- 1 cup tomato sauce (homemade or good quality store-bought)
- 8 ounces fresh mozzarella, sliced
- Prosciutto slices
- Handful of fresh arugula
- Extra-virgin olive oil
- Salt and pepper to taste
- Grated Parmesan cheese (optional)
- Cornmeal or flour for dusting

Instructions:

Preheat the Oven:
- Preheat your oven to the highest temperature it can go, typically around 475-500°F (245-260°C).

Prepare the Dough:
- If using store-bought dough, follow the package instructions for bringing it to room temperature. If making homemade dough, roll it out on a floured surface to your desired thickness.

Prepare the Pizza Peel or Pan:
- If using a pizza stone, sprinkle some cornmeal on a pizza peel. If using a baking sheet, lightly grease it or dust it with flour.

Assemble the Pizza:
- Place the rolled-out dough on the pizza peel or prepared baking sheet.
- Spread the tomato sauce evenly over the dough, leaving a small border around the edges.
- Arrange the fresh mozzarella slices on top of the sauce.
- Drape slices of prosciutto over the mozzarella.

Bake the Pizza:
- If using a pizza stone, carefully transfer the pizza to the preheated stone in the oven. If using a baking sheet, simply place it in the oven.
- Bake for about 10-12 minutes or until the crust is golden and the cheese is melted and slightly bubbly.

Add Arugula and Finish:
- Once out of the oven, immediately scatter a handful of fresh arugula over the hot pizza.
- Drizzle extra-virgin olive oil over the top.
- Optionally, sprinkle with grated Parmesan cheese for added flavor.

Slice and Serve:
- Let the pizza cool for a minute, then slice it into wedges or squares.
- Serve immediately, and enjoy the perfect balance of flavors with the salty prosciutto and peppery arugula!

Feel free to customize the recipe by adding a squeeze of lemon juice to the arugula or a dash of balsamic glaze for extra depth of flavor.

Truffle Oil Margherita

Ingredients:

- Pizza dough (store-bought or homemade)
- 1 cup tomato sauce (homemade or good quality store-bought)
- 8 ounces fresh mozzarella, sliced
- Fresh basil leaves
- Truffle oil
- Salt and pepper to taste
- Grated Parmesan cheese (optional)
- Cornmeal or flour for dusting

Instructions:

Preheat the Oven:
- Preheat your oven to the highest temperature it can go, typically around 475-500°F (245-260°C).

Prepare the Dough:
- If using store-bought dough, follow the package instructions for bringing it to room temperature. If making homemade dough, roll it out on a floured surface to your desired thickness.

Prepare the Pizza Peel or Pan:
- If using a pizza stone, sprinkle some cornmeal on a pizza peel. If using a baking sheet, lightly grease it or dust it with flour.

Assemble the Pizza:
- Place the rolled-out dough on the pizza peel or prepared baking sheet.
- Spread the tomato sauce evenly over the dough, leaving a small border around the edges.
- Arrange the fresh mozzarella slices on top of the sauce.
- Drizzle truffle oil over the entire pizza, focusing on the cheese and around the edges.
- Season with a pinch of salt and pepper.

Bake the Pizza:
- If using a pizza stone, carefully transfer the pizza to the preheated stone in the oven. If using a baking sheet, simply place it in the oven.
- Bake for about 10-12 minutes or until the crust is golden and the cheese is melted and slightly bubbly.

Finish with Fresh Basil and Parmesan:

- Once out of the oven, immediately scatter fresh basil leaves over the hot pizza.
- Optionally, sprinkle with grated Parmesan cheese for added richness.

Slice and Serve:
- Let the pizza cool for a minute, then slice it into wedges or squares.
- Serve immediately and savor the decadent aroma and flavor of truffle-infused Margherita pizza!

Feel free to customize by adding a drizzle of balsamic glaze or a handful of arugula for additional depth of flavor and texture.

Regional Pizza Styles:

Neapolitan Pizza

Ingredients:

- Pizza dough (Neapolitan-style, made with high-protein flour)
- San Marzano tomatoes (crushed or pureed)
- Fresh mozzarella cheese, preferably Fior di Latte or Buffalo Mozzarella
- Fresh basil leaves
- Extra-virgin olive oil
- Salt

Instructions:

Preheat the Oven:
- If you have a pizza stone or a pizza oven, preheat it to the highest temperature it can reach, ideally around 800°F (425°C). The high heat is crucial for achieving the characteristic Neapolitan crust.

Prepare the Dough:
- Use Neapolitan-style pizza dough made with high-protein flour. Roll out the dough on a floured surface, forming a thin, 12-inch (30 cm) round shape. Leave the edges slightly thicker for the characteristic puffy crust.

Prepare the Pizza Peel:
- Dust a pizza peel with flour or semolina to prevent sticking.

Assemble the Pizza:
- Place the rolled-out dough onto the prepared pizza peel.
- Spread a thin layer of crushed or pureed San Marzano tomatoes over the dough, leaving a border around the edges.
- Tear pieces of fresh mozzarella and distribute them evenly over the sauce.
- Sprinkle with a pinch of salt.
- Add fresh basil leaves on top.

Bake the Pizza:
- If using a pizza stone, carefully transfer the pizza onto the preheated stone in the oven. If using a pizza oven, slide the pizza directly onto the oven floor.
- Bake for about 90 seconds to 2 minutes, or until the crust is puffed up, golden, and the cheese is melted and bubbly.

Finish with Olive Oil:
- Once out of the oven, drizzle extra-virgin olive oil over the hot pizza.

Slice and Serve:
- Allow the pizza to cool for a minute, then slice it into wedges.
- Serve immediately, and enjoy the authentic taste of Neapolitan Pizza!

Remember, Neapolitan pizza is all about simplicity and using the best-quality ingredients. If you can, try to use a wood-fired oven for the most authentic Neapolitan pizza experience. Adjust the toppings and quantities to suit your preferences. Buon appetito!

Roman Pizza (Pizza al Taglio)

Ingredients:

For the Pizza Dough:

- 4 cups all-purpose flour
- 2 teaspoons active dry yeast
- 1 1/2 cups warm water
- 2 tablespoons olive oil
- 1 teaspoon sugar
- 1 teaspoon salt

For the Toppings:

- Tomato sauce (homemade or good quality store-bought)
- Fresh mozzarella, shredded or sliced
- Provolone or Pecorino Romano cheese, grated
- Fresh basil leaves
- Olive oil
- Salt and pepper to taste

Instructions:

Prepare the Dough:
- In a bowl, combine warm water, sugar, and active dry yeast. Let it sit for about 5 minutes until it becomes frothy.
- In a large mixing bowl, combine the flour and salt. Make a well in the center and pour in the yeast mixture and olive oil.
- Mix until a dough forms, then knead on a floured surface for about 8-10 minutes until smooth.
- Place the dough in a lightly oiled bowl, cover with a damp cloth, and let it rise in a warm place for about 1 to 1.5 hours, or until it doubles in size.

Preheat the Oven:
- Preheat your oven to 450°F (230°C).

Prepare the Baking Pan:
- Grease a rectangular baking pan with olive oil. The size can vary, but a common size is around 13x18 inches.

Shape the Dough:

- Once the dough has risen, gently punch it down and transfer it to the greased baking pan. Press the dough evenly into the pan, making sure to reach the edges.

Top the Pizza:
- Spread a layer of tomato sauce over the dough, leaving a small border.
- Sprinkle the shredded or sliced fresh mozzarella over the sauce.
- Add grated Provolone or Pecorino Romano cheese.
- Scatter fresh basil leaves over the top.
- Drizzle with olive oil and season with salt and pepper.

Bake the Pizza:
- Bake in the preheated oven for about 20-25 minutes or until the crust is golden and the cheese is melted and bubbly.

Slice and Serve:
- Once out of the oven, let it cool for a few minutes before slicing it into squares or rectangles.
- Serve warm and enjoy the deliciousness of Roman Pizza al Taglio!

Feel free to customize the toppings based on your preferences. This pizza is great for gatherings as it can be sliced into smaller portions for sharing. Buon appetito!

Sicilian Pizza

Ingredients:

For the Pizza Dough:

- 4 cups bread flour
- 1 1/2 teaspoons active dry yeast
- 1 1/2 cups warm water
- 2 tablespoons olive oil
- 1 teaspoon sugar
- 1 1/2 teaspoons salt

For the Pizza Sauce:

- 1 can (28 oz) whole peeled tomatoes
- 2 cloves garlic, minced
- 1 teaspoon dried oregano
- 1 teaspoon dried basil
- Salt and pepper to taste
- Olive oil

For the Toppings:

- 2 cups shredded mozzarella cheese
- Grated Parmesan cheese
- Optional: Sliced pepperoni, cooked sausage, olives, mushrooms, etc.

Instructions:

Prepare the Dough:

> In a bowl, combine warm water, sugar, and active dry yeast. Let it sit for about 5 minutes until it becomes frothy.
> In a large mixing bowl, combine bread flour and salt. Make a well in the center and pour in the yeast mixture and olive oil.
> Mix until a dough forms, then knead on a floured surface for about 8-10 minutes until smooth.
> Place the dough in a lightly oiled bowl, cover with a damp cloth, and let it rise in a warm place for about 1.5 to 2 hours, or until it doubles in size.

Prepare the Pizza Sauce:

> In a blender or food processor, combine the whole peeled tomatoes, minced garlic, dried oregano, dried basil, salt, and pepper.
> Blend until smooth. You can adjust the seasoning to your taste.
> Heat a bit of olive oil in a saucepan and add the tomato mixture. Simmer for about 15-20 minutes until it thickens slightly.

Assemble and Bake:

> Preheat your oven to 450°F (230°C).
> Grease a rectangular baking pan (usually around 13x18 inches) with olive oil.
> Press the risen dough into the prepared pan, covering the entire surface. If it resists, let it rest for a few minutes and then continue.
> Spread the pizza sauce over the dough, leaving a small border.
> Sprinkle the shredded mozzarella evenly over the sauce.
> Add any additional toppings of your choice, such as pepperoni, sausage, olives, etc.
> Grate Parmesan cheese over the top.
> Bake in the preheated oven for about 20-25 minutes or until the crust is golden, and the cheese is melted and bubbly.
> Once out of the oven, let it cool for a few minutes before slicing it into squares.
> Serve warm and enjoy the deliciousness of Sicilian Pizza!

Sicilian pizza is known for its thick crust and hearty toppings, making it a satisfying and flavorful option. Feel free to experiment with toppings to suit your taste preferences. Buon appetito!

Calzone Napoletano

Ingredients:

For the Pizza Dough:

- 4 cups all-purpose flour
- 2 1/4 teaspoons active dry yeast
- 1 1/2 cups warm water
- 2 tablespoons olive oil
- 1 teaspoon sugar
- 1 teaspoon salt

For the Filling:

- 1 cup ricotta cheese
- 1 cup shredded mozzarella cheese
- 1/2 cup grated Parmesan cheese
- 1 cup cooked ham or salami, diced
- 1 cup cooked spinach, squeezed dry and chopped
- 1/4 cup fresh basil, chopped
- Salt and pepper to taste
- Olive oil for brushing

For Assembling:

- Cornmeal or flour for dusting

Instructions:

Prepare the Dough:

In a bowl, combine warm water, sugar, and active dry yeast. Let it sit for about 5 minutes until it becomes frothy.

In a large mixing bowl, combine all-purpose flour and salt. Make a well in the center and pour in the yeast mixture and olive oil.

Mix until a dough forms, then knead on a floured surface for about 8-10 minutes until smooth.

Place the dough in a lightly oiled bowl, cover with a damp cloth, and let it rise in a warm place for about 1.5 to 2 hours, or until it doubles in size.

Prepare the Filling:

In a mixing bowl, combine ricotta cheese, shredded mozzarella, Parmesan, diced ham or salami, chopped spinach, fresh basil, salt, and pepper. Mix well.

Assemble and Bake:

Preheat your oven to 475°F (245°C). If you have a pizza stone, place it in the oven while preheating.
Punch down the risen dough and divide it into two equal portions.
On a floured surface, roll out each portion of dough into a circle, about 12 inches in diameter.
Place half of the filling on one side of each dough circle, leaving a border around the edges.
Fold the other half of the dough over the filling, creating a half-moon shape.
Seal the edges of the calzones by pressing them with your fingers or using a fork.
If using a pizza stone, transfer the calzones to a pizza peel dusted with cornmeal or flour.
If using a baking sheet, place the calzones directly on it.
Brush the tops of the calzones with olive oil.
Bake in the preheated oven for about 15-20 minutes or until the calzones are golden brown.
Once out of the oven, let them cool for a few minutes before slicing.
Serve warm and enjoy the deliciousness of Calzone Napoletano!

Calzone Napoletano is a delightful and portable way to enjoy the flavors of pizza. Feel free to customize the filling with your favorite ingredients. Buon appetito!

Focaccia Barese

Ingredients:

For the Focaccia Dough:

- 4 cups all-purpose flour
- 2 teaspoons active dry yeast
- 1 1/2 cups warm water
- 2 tablespoons olive oil
- 1 teaspoon sugar
- 1 1/2 teaspoons salt

For the Topping:

- Cherry tomatoes, halved
- Black olives, pitted and halved
- Fresh rosemary, chopped
- Coarse sea salt
- Extra-virgin olive oil

Instructions:

Prepare the Focaccia Dough:

In a bowl, combine warm water, sugar, and active dry yeast. Let it sit for about 5 minutes until it becomes frothy.

In a large mixing bowl, combine all-purpose flour and salt. Make a well in the center and pour in the yeast mixture and olive oil.

Mix until a dough forms, then knead on a floured surface for about 8-10 minutes until smooth.

Place the dough in a lightly oiled bowl, cover with a damp cloth, and let it rise in a warm place for about 1.5 to 2 hours, or until it doubles in size.

Assemble and Bake:

Preheat your oven to 425°F (220°C). If you have a baking stone, place it in the oven while preheating.

Punch down the risen dough and transfer it to a parchment-lined baking sheet.

Using your fingertips, press the dough to flatten it, spreading it evenly across the baking sheet.

Drizzle the top of the dough with extra-virgin olive oil and use your fingers to create dimples in the surface.

Arrange halved cherry tomatoes and black olives on the dough. Sprinkle chopped fresh rosemary and coarse sea salt over the top.

If using a baking stone, carefully transfer the parchment paper with the focaccia onto the preheated stone in the oven. If using a baking sheet, place it directly in the oven.

Bake for about 20-25 minutes or until the focaccia is golden brown and cooked through.

Once out of the oven, drizzle a bit more extra-virgin olive oil over the top.

Allow the focaccia to cool slightly before slicing.

Serve warm and enjoy the wonderful taste and texture of Focaccia Barese!

Focaccia Barese is often enjoyed on its own or as a side dish to accompany meals. Feel free to experiment with additional toppings, such as garlic, onions, or different herbs, to suit your preferences. Buon appetito!

Seafood Pizzas:

Pizza Frutti di Mare

Ingredients:

For the Pizza Dough:

- 4 cups all-purpose flour
- 2 1/4 teaspoons active dry yeast
- 1 1/2 cups warm water
- 2 tablespoons olive oil
- 1 teaspoon sugar
- 1 1/2 teaspoons salt

For the Pizza Sauce:

- 1 can (28 oz) whole peeled tomatoes
- 2 cloves garlic, minced
- 1 teaspoon dried oregano
- 1 teaspoon dried basil
- Salt and pepper to taste
- Olive oil

For the Seafood Toppings:

- 1/2 pound shrimp, peeled and deveined
- 1/2 pound mussels, cleaned and debearded
- 1/2 pound clams, cleaned
- 1/2 pound calamari, cleaned and sliced into rings
- Olive oil
- Garlic, minced
- Red pepper flakes (optional)
- Fresh parsley, chopped
- Lemon wedges for serving

For the Cheese:

- 8 ounces fresh mozzarella, sliced

- Grated Parmesan cheese

Instructions:

Prepare the Pizza Dough:

In a bowl, combine warm water, sugar, and active dry yeast. Let it sit for about 5 minutes until it becomes frothy.

In a large mixing bowl, combine all-purpose flour and salt. Make a well in the center and pour in the yeast mixture and olive oil.

Mix until a dough forms, then knead on a floured surface for about 8-10 minutes until smooth.

Place the dough in a lightly oiled bowl, cover with a damp cloth, and let it rise in a warm place for about 1.5 to 2 hours, or until it doubles in size.

Prepare the Pizza Sauce:

In a blender or food processor, combine the whole peeled tomatoes, minced garlic, dried oregano, dried basil, salt, and pepper.

Blend until smooth. Adjust the seasoning to your taste.

Heat a bit of olive oil in a saucepan and add the tomato mixture. Simmer for about 15-20 minutes until it thickens slightly.

Prepare the Seafood:

In a pan, heat olive oil over medium heat. Add minced garlic and red pepper flakes (if using) and sauté for a minute.

Add the shrimp, mussels, clams, and calamari to the pan. Cook until the seafood is just cooked through. Set aside.

Assemble and Bake:

Preheat your oven to 475°F (245°C). If you have a pizza stone, place it in the oven while preheating.

Punch down the risen dough and divide it into two equal portions.

On a floured surface, roll out each portion of dough into a circle, about 12 inches in diameter.

Place each rolled-out dough on a parchment-lined pizza peel or baking sheet.

Spread a layer of the tomato sauce over each pizza dough.

Arrange the cooked seafood evenly over the sauce.
Place fresh mozzarella slices on top of the seafood.
Sprinkle grated Parmesan cheese over the pizzas.
If using a pizza stone, carefully transfer the parchment paper with the pizza onto the preheated stone in the oven. If using a baking sheet, place the pizzas directly on it.
Bake for about 15-20 minutes or until the crust is golden and the cheese is melted and bubbly.
Once out of the oven, sprinkle fresh parsley over the top.
Serve warm with lemon wedges on the side.

Enjoy the delightful flavors of Pizza Frutti di Mare, showcasing the freshness of seafood on a delicious pizza!

Calamari and Lemon Pizza

Ingredients:

For the Pizza Dough:

- 4 cups all-purpose flour
- 2 teaspoons active dry yeast
- 1 1/2 cups warm water
- 2 tablespoons olive oil
- 1 teaspoon sugar
- 1 teaspoon salt

For the Toppings:

- 1 cup tomato sauce (homemade or good quality store-bought)
- 8 ounces fresh mozzarella, sliced
- 1 cup cleaned and sliced calamari rings
- Zest of one lemon
- Juice of half a lemon
- 2 tablespoons capers, drained
- 2 tablespoons chopped fresh parsley
- Red pepper flakes (optional)
- Salt and black pepper to taste
- Extra-virgin olive oil for drizzling

Instructions:

Prepare the Pizza Dough:

> In a bowl, combine warm water, sugar, and active dry yeast. Let it sit for about 5 minutes until it becomes frothy.
> In a large mixing bowl, combine all-purpose flour and salt. Make a well in the center and pour in the yeast mixture and olive oil.
> Mix until a dough forms, then knead on a floured surface for about 8-10 minutes until smooth.
> Place the dough in a lightly oiled bowl, cover with a damp cloth, and let it rise in a warm place for about 1.5 to 2 hours, or until it doubles in size.

Assemble and Bake:

Preheat your oven to 475°F (245°C). If you have a pizza stone, place it in the oven while preheating.

Roll out the risen dough on a floured surface to your desired thickness.

Transfer the rolled-out dough to a pizza peel or parchment paper if using a baking sheet.

Spread a layer of tomato sauce evenly over the dough, leaving a small border around the edges.

Arrange the fresh mozzarella slices on top of the sauce.

Distribute the sliced calamari over the pizza.

Sprinkle lemon zest over the pizza, and drizzle the lemon juice evenly.

Add capers and chopped fresh parsley.

Season with salt and black pepper to taste. If you like some heat, sprinkle red pepper flakes.

If using a pizza stone, carefully transfer the pizza to the preheated stone in the oven. If using a baking sheet, place it directly in the oven.

Bake for about 12-15 minutes or until the crust is golden, the cheese is melted, and the calamari is cooked.

Once out of the oven, drizzle extra-virgin olive oil over the top.

Allow the pizza to cool for a minute, then slice and serve.

Enjoy the unique and delicious flavor combination of Calamari and Lemon Pizza!

Feel free to customize the recipe by adding other seafood like shrimp or mussels, and adjust the toppings to suit your taste preferences. Buon appetito!

Shrimp Scampi Pizza

Ingredients:

For the Pizza Dough:

- 4 cups all-purpose flour
- 2 teaspoons active dry yeast
- 1 1/2 cups warm water
- 2 tablespoons olive oil
- 1 teaspoon sugar
- 1 teaspoon salt

For the Shrimp Scampi Topping:

- 1 pound large shrimp, peeled and deveined
- 4 tablespoons unsalted butter
- 4 cloves garlic, minced
- 1/4 cup white wine
- Juice of 1 lemon
- Zest of 1 lemon
- 1/4 cup chopped fresh parsley
- Salt and black pepper to taste

For the Pizza Assembly:

- Olive oil for drizzling
- 8 ounces shredded mozzarella cheese
- Grated Parmesan cheese
- Red pepper flakes (optional)
- Fresh parsley for garnish

Instructions:

Prepare the Pizza Dough:

In a bowl, combine warm water, sugar, and active dry yeast. Let it sit for about 5 minutes until it becomes frothy.

In a large mixing bowl, combine all-purpose flour and salt. Make a well in the center and pour in the yeast mixture and olive oil.

Mix until a dough forms, then knead on a floured surface for about 8-10 minutes until smooth.

Place the dough in a lightly oiled bowl, cover with a damp cloth, and let it rise in a warm place for about 1.5 to 2 hours, or until it doubles in size.

Prepare the Shrimp Scampi Topping:

In a skillet over medium heat, melt the butter.

Add minced garlic and sauté for about 1-2 minutes until fragrant.

Add the shrimp to the skillet and cook until they turn pink, about 2-3 minutes per side.

Pour in the white wine, lemon juice, and lemon zest. Allow it to simmer for an additional 2-3 minutes.

Season with salt and black pepper to taste. Stir in chopped fresh parsley.

Remove the skillet from heat and set aside.

Assemble and Bake the Pizza:

Preheat your oven to 475°F (245°C). If you have a pizza stone, place it in the oven while preheating.

Roll out the risen dough on a floured surface to your desired thickness.

Transfer the rolled-out dough to a pizza peel or parchment paper if using a baking sheet.

Drizzle olive oil over the dough.

Sprinkle shredded mozzarella cheese evenly over the dough.

Distribute the shrimp scampi mixture evenly over the pizza.

Grate Parmesan cheese over the top.

If you like a bit of heat, sprinkle red pepper flakes over the pizza.

If using a pizza stone, carefully transfer the pizza to the preheated stone in the oven. If using a baking sheet, place it directly in the oven.

Bake for about 12-15 minutes or until the crust is golden, the cheese is melted, and the shrimp are cooked.

Once out of the oven, garnish with fresh parsley.

Allow the pizza to cool for a minute, then slice and serve.

Enjoy the deliciousness of Shrimp Scampi Pizza!

Feel free to customize the recipe by adding additional toppings such as cherry tomatoes, artichoke hearts, or spinach. Buon appetito!

Vegetarian Pizzas:

Rustic Eggplant and Ricotta Pizza

Ingredients:

For the Pizza Dough:

- 4 cups all-purpose flour
- 2 teaspoons active dry yeast
- 1 1/2 cups warm water
- 2 tablespoons olive oil
- 1 teaspoon sugar
- 1 teaspoon salt

For the Toppings:

- 1 medium-sized eggplant, thinly sliced
- 1 cup ricotta cheese
- 1/2 cup grated Parmesan cheese
- 1/4 cup fresh basil, chopped
- 2 cloves garlic, minced
- Salt and black pepper to taste
- Extra-virgin olive oil for drizzling

Instructions:

Prepare the Pizza Dough:

In a bowl, combine warm water, sugar, and active dry yeast. Let it sit for about 5 minutes until it becomes frothy.

In a large mixing bowl, combine all-purpose flour and salt. Make a well in the center and pour in the yeast mixture and olive oil.

Mix until a dough forms, then knead on a floured surface for about 8-10 minutes until smooth.

Place the dough in a lightly oiled bowl, cover with a damp cloth, and let it rise in a warm place for about 1.5 to 2 hours, or until it doubles in size.

Assemble and Bake:

Preheat your oven to 475°F (245°C). If you have a pizza stone, place it in the oven while preheating.

Roll out the risen dough on a floured surface to your desired thickness.

Transfer the rolled-out dough to a pizza peel or parchment paper if using a baking sheet.

In a skillet, sauté the thinly sliced eggplant with a bit of olive oil until softened and lightly browned. Season with salt and black pepper.

Spread the ricotta cheese evenly over the pizza dough, leaving a small border around the edges.

Arrange the sautéed eggplant slices on top of the ricotta.

Sprinkle grated Parmesan cheese over the pizza.

Scatter minced garlic and chopped fresh basil on top.

Drizzle the entire pizza with extra-virgin olive oil.

If using a pizza stone, carefully transfer the pizza to the preheated stone in the oven. If using a baking sheet, place it directly in the oven.

Bake for about 12-15 minutes or until the crust is golden and the cheese is melted.

Once out of the oven, drizzle a bit more extra-virgin olive oil over the top.

Allow the pizza to cool for a minute, then slice and serve.

Enjoy the rustic goodness of Eggplant and Ricotta Pizza!

Feel free to add a sprinkle of red pepper flakes for a hint of heat or experiment with other toppings to suit your taste. Buon appetito!

Mushroom Trifolati Pizza

Ingredients:

For the Pizza Dough:

- 4 cups all-purpose flour
- 2 teaspoons active dry yeast
- 1 1/2 cups warm water
- 2 tablespoons olive oil
- 1 teaspoon sugar
- 1 teaspoon salt

For the Mushroom Trifolati:

- 2 tablespoons olive oil
- 1 pound (about 450g) mixed mushrooms (cremini, shiitake, oyster), cleaned and sliced
- 2 cloves garlic, minced
- 1 teaspoon fresh thyme leaves
- Salt and black pepper to taste
- 1/4 cup dry white wine (optional)
- Fresh parsley, chopped (for garnish)

For the Pizza Toppings:

- 1 cup shredded mozzarella cheese
- 1/2 cup grated Parmesan cheese
- 1/2 cup ricotta cheese
- Salt and black pepper to taste
- Extra-virgin olive oil for drizzling

Instructions:

Prepare the Pizza Dough:

> In a bowl, combine warm water, sugar, and active dry yeast. Let it sit for about 5 minutes until it becomes frothy.
> In a large mixing bowl, combine all-purpose flour and salt. Make a well in the center and pour in the yeast mixture and olive oil.

Mix until a dough forms, then knead on a floured surface for about 8-10 minutes until smooth.

Place the dough in a lightly oiled bowl, cover with a damp cloth, and let it rise in a warm place for about 1.5 to 2 hours, or until it doubles in size.

Prepare the Mushroom Trifolati:

In a skillet, heat olive oil over medium heat. Add minced garlic and sauté for about 1 minute until fragrant.

Add sliced mushrooms and thyme to the skillet. Cook, stirring occasionally, until the mushrooms release their moisture and become golden brown.

Season with salt and black pepper to taste. If using, add the white wine and cook until it evaporates.

Remove the skillet from heat, and set the mushroom trifolati aside.

Assemble and Bake:

Preheat your oven to 475°F (245°C). If you have a pizza stone, place it in the oven while preheating.

Roll out the risen dough on a floured surface to your desired thickness.

Transfer the rolled-out dough to a pizza peel or parchment paper if using a baking sheet.

Spread ricotta cheese evenly over the pizza dough, leaving a small border around the edges.

Sprinkle shredded mozzarella cheese over the ricotta.

Spoon the mushroom trifolati mixture evenly over the cheese.

Sprinkle grated Parmesan cheese on top.

Season with salt and black pepper to taste.

If using a pizza stone, carefully transfer the pizza to the preheated stone in the oven. If using a baking sheet, place it directly in the oven.

Bake for about 12-15 minutes or until the crust is golden and the cheese is melted.

Once out of the oven, drizzle extra-virgin olive oil over the top and garnish with chopped fresh parsley.

Allow the pizza to cool for a minute, then slice and serve.

Enjoy the savory goodness of Mushroom Trifolati Pizza!

Feel free to customize by adding a sprinkle of red pepper flakes for some heat or experimenting with different mushroom varieties. Buon appetito!

Zucchini and Pesto Pizza

Ingredients:

For the Pizza Dough:

- 4 cups all-purpose flour
- 2 teaspoons active dry yeast
- 1 1/2 cups warm water
- 2 tablespoons olive oil
- 1 teaspoon sugar
- 1 teaspoon salt

For the Pesto:

- 2 cups fresh basil leaves, packed
- 1/2 cup grated Parmesan cheese
- 1/3 cup pine nuts
- 2 cloves garlic, minced
- 1/2 cup extra-virgin olive oil
- Salt and black pepper to taste

For the Pizza Toppings:

- 1 medium zucchini, thinly sliced
- 1 cup shredded mozzarella cheese
- 1/4 cup crumbled feta cheese
- Extra-virgin olive oil for drizzling
- Red pepper flakes (optional)

Instructions:

Prepare the Pizza Dough:

> In a bowl, combine warm water, sugar, and active dry yeast. Let it sit for about 5 minutes until it becomes frothy.
> In a large mixing bowl, combine all-purpose flour and salt. Make a well in the center and pour in the yeast mixture and olive oil.
> Mix until a dough forms, then knead on a floured surface for about 8-10 minutes until smooth.

Place the dough in a lightly oiled bowl, cover with a damp cloth, and let it rise in a warm place for about 1.5 to 2 hours, or until it doubles in size.

Prepare the Pesto:

In a food processor, combine basil, Parmesan cheese, pine nuts, and minced garlic. Pulse until finely chopped.
With the food processor running, gradually add the olive oil until the pesto reaches your desired consistency.
Season with salt and black pepper to taste. Set aside.

Assemble and Bake:

Preheat your oven to 475°F (245°C). If you have a pizza stone, place it in the oven while preheating.
Roll out the risen dough on a floured surface to your desired thickness.
Transfer the rolled-out dough to a pizza peel or parchment paper if using a baking sheet.
Spread a generous layer of the prepared pesto over the pizza dough, leaving a small border around the edges.
Sprinkle shredded mozzarella cheese over the pesto.
Arrange thinly sliced zucchini evenly over the cheese.
Crumble feta cheese over the zucchini.
Drizzle the entire pizza with extra-virgin olive oil.
If using a pizza stone, carefully transfer the pizza to the preheated stone in the oven. If using a baking sheet, place it directly in the oven.
Bake for about 12-15 minutes or until the crust is golden and the cheese is melted.
Once out of the oven, drizzle a bit more extra-virgin olive oil over the top.
If desired, sprinkle with red pepper flakes for a hint of heat.
Allow the pizza to cool for a minute, then slice and serve.
Enjoy the delightful combination of Zucchini and Pesto Pizza!

Feel free to add additional toppings such as cherry tomatoes, red onions, or arugula for extra freshness and flavor. Buon appetito!

Artichoke and Spinach Pizza

Ingredients:

For the Pizza Dough:

- 4 cups all-purpose flour
- 2 teaspoons active dry yeast
- 1 1/2 cups warm water
- 2 tablespoons olive oil
- 1 teaspoon sugar
- 1 teaspoon salt

For the Pizza Sauce:

- 1 cup tomato sauce (homemade or good quality store-bought)
- 2 cloves garlic, minced
- 1 teaspoon dried oregano
- Salt and black pepper to taste

For the Toppings:

- 1 cup shredded mozzarella cheese
- 1 cup fresh spinach, chopped
- 1 cup marinated artichoke hearts, drained and chopped
- 1/2 cup grated Parmesan cheese
- 1/4 cup crumbled feta cheese
- Red pepper flakes (optional)
- Extra-virgin olive oil for drizzling

Instructions:

Prepare the Pizza Dough:

> In a bowl, combine warm water, sugar, and active dry yeast. Let it sit for about 5 minutes until it becomes frothy.
> In a large mixing bowl, combine all-purpose flour and salt. Make a well in the center and pour in the yeast mixture and olive oil.
> Mix until a dough forms, then knead on a floured surface for about 8-10 minutes until smooth.

Place the dough in a lightly oiled bowl, cover with a damp cloth, and let it rise in a warm place for about 1.5 to 2 hours, or until it doubles in size.

Prepare the Pizza Sauce:

In a small bowl, mix together tomato sauce, minced garlic, dried oregano, salt, and black pepper. Set aside.

Assemble and Bake:

Preheat your oven to 475°F (245°C). If you have a pizza stone, place it in the oven while preheating.
Roll out the risen dough on a floured surface to your desired thickness.
Transfer the rolled-out dough to a pizza peel or parchment paper if using a baking sheet.
Spread the prepared pizza sauce evenly over the dough, leaving a small border around the edges.
Sprinkle shredded mozzarella cheese over the sauce.
Distribute chopped fresh spinach and chopped artichoke hearts evenly over the pizza.
Sprinkle grated Parmesan and crumbled feta cheese on top.
If desired, add red pepper flakes for a bit of heat.
Drizzle the entire pizza with extra-virgin olive oil.
If using a pizza stone, carefully transfer the pizza to the preheated stone in the oven. If using a baking sheet, place it directly in the oven.
Bake for about 12-15 minutes or until the crust is golden and the cheese is melted.
Once out of the oven, let it cool for a minute, then slice and serve.
Enjoy the delightful combination of Artichoke and Spinach Pizza!

Feel free to customize by adding garlic, caramelized onions, or black olives for additional flavor. Buon appetito!

Meat Lover's Pizzas:

Quattro Carni Pizza

Ingredients:

For the Pizza Dough:

- 4 cups all-purpose flour
- 2 teaspoons active dry yeast
- 1 1/2 cups warm water
- 2 tablespoons olive oil
- 1 teaspoon sugar
- 1 teaspoon salt

For the Pizza Sauce:

- 1 cup tomato sauce (homemade or good quality store-bought)
- 2 cloves garlic, minced
- 1 teaspoon dried oregano
- Salt and black pepper to taste

For the Toppings:

- 1/2 cup cooked and crumbled Italian sausage
- 1/2 cup pepperoni slices
- 1/2 cup cooked and shredded chicken
- 1/2 cup cooked and crumbled bacon
- 1 cup shredded mozzarella cheese
- 1/4 cup grated Parmesan cheese
- Fresh basil leaves (for garnish, optional)
- Red pepper flakes (optional)
- Extra-virgin olive oil for drizzling

Instructions:

Prepare the Pizza Dough:

> In a bowl, combine warm water, sugar, and active dry yeast. Let it sit for about 5 minutes until it becomes frothy.

In a large mixing bowl, combine all-purpose flour and salt. Make a well in the center and pour in the yeast mixture and olive oil.

Mix until a dough forms, then knead on a floured surface for about 8-10 minutes until smooth.

Place the dough in a lightly oiled bowl, cover with a damp cloth, and let it rise in a warm place for about 1.5 to 2 hours, or until it doubles in size.

Prepare the Pizza Sauce:

In a small bowl, mix together tomato sauce, minced garlic, dried oregano, salt, and black pepper. Set aside.

Assemble and Bake:

Preheat your oven to 475°F (245°C). If you have a pizza stone, place it in the oven while preheating.

Roll out the risen dough on a floured surface to your desired thickness.

Transfer the rolled-out dough to a pizza peel or parchment paper if using a baking sheet.

Spread the prepared pizza sauce evenly over the dough, leaving a small border around the edges.

Sprinkle shredded mozzarella cheese over the sauce.

Distribute cooked and crumbled Italian sausage, pepperoni slices, shredded chicken, and crumbled bacon evenly over the pizza.

Sprinkle grated Parmesan cheese on top.

If desired, add red pepper flakes for a bit of heat.

If using a pizza stone, carefully transfer the pizza to the preheated stone in the oven. If using a baking sheet, place it directly in the oven.

Bake for about 12-15 minutes or until the crust is golden and the cheese is melted.

Once out of the oven, let it cool for a minute, then garnish with fresh basil leaves and drizzle with extra-virgin olive oil.

Slice and serve the delicious Quattro Carni Pizza!

Feel free to customize the meat choices or add other favorite meats to suit your taste. Buon appetito!

Spicy Soppressata Pizza

Ingredients:

For the Pizza Dough:

- 4 cups all-purpose flour
- 2 teaspoons active dry yeast
- 1 1/2 cups warm water
- 2 tablespoons olive oil
- 1 teaspoon sugar
- 1 teaspoon salt

For the Pizza Sauce:

- 1 cup tomato sauce (homemade or good quality store-bought)
- 2 cloves garlic, minced
- 1 teaspoon dried oregano
- 1/2 teaspoon red pepper flakes (adjust to taste)
- Salt and black pepper to taste

For the Toppings:

- 1 cup shredded mozzarella cheese
- 1/2 cup grated Parmesan cheese
- 1/2 cup sliced spicy soppressata
- 1/4 cup sliced black olives
- Fresh basil leaves (for garnish, optional)
- Extra-virgin olive oil for drizzling

Instructions:

Prepare the Pizza Dough:

> In a bowl, combine warm water, sugar, and active dry yeast. Let it sit for about 5 minutes until it becomes frothy.
> In a large mixing bowl, combine all-purpose flour and salt. Make a well in the center and pour in the yeast mixture and olive oil.

Mix until a dough forms, then knead on a floured surface for about 8-10 minutes until smooth.

Place the dough in a lightly oiled bowl, cover with a damp cloth, and let it rise in a warm place for about 1.5 to 2 hours, or until it doubles in size.

Prepare the Pizza Sauce:

In a small bowl, mix together tomato sauce, minced garlic, dried oregano, red pepper flakes, salt, and black pepper. Set aside.

Assemble and Bake:

Preheat your oven to 475°F (245°C). If you have a pizza stone, place it in the oven while preheating.

Roll out the risen dough on a floured surface to your desired thickness.

Transfer the rolled-out dough to a pizza peel or parchment paper if using a baking sheet.

Spread the prepared pizza sauce evenly over the dough, leaving a small border around the edges.

Sprinkle shredded mozzarella cheese over the sauce.

Distribute slices of spicy soppressata and black olives evenly over the pizza.

Sprinkle grated Parmesan cheese on top.

If desired, add extra red pepper flakes for more heat.

If using a pizza stone, carefully transfer the pizza to the preheated stone in the oven. If using a baking sheet, place it directly in the oven.

Bake for about 12-15 minutes or until the crust is golden and the cheese is melted.

Once out of the oven, let it cool for a minute, then garnish with fresh basil leaves and drizzle with extra-virgin olive oil.

Slice and enjoy the bold and spicy flavors of Spicy Soppressata Pizza!

Feel free to customize the spice level by adjusting the amount of red pepper flakes or adding your favorite spicy ingredients. Buon appetito!

Bolognese Pizza

Ingredients:

For the Pizza Dough:

- 4 cups all-purpose flour
- 2 teaspoons active dry yeast
- 1 1/2 cups warm water
- 2 tablespoons olive oil
- 1 teaspoon sugar
- 1 teaspoon salt

For the Bolognese Sauce:

- 1 pound ground beef
- 1/2 cup finely diced onion
- 1/2 cup finely diced carrot
- 1/2 cup finely diced celery
- 2 cloves garlic, minced
- 1 cup tomato sauce
- 1/2 cup red wine (optional)
- 1 teaspoon dried oregano
- 1 teaspoon dried basil
- Salt and black pepper to taste

For the Pizza Toppings:

- 1 cup shredded mozzarella cheese
- 1/2 cup grated Parmesan cheese
- Fresh basil leaves (for garnish, optional)
- Red pepper flakes (optional)
- Extra-virgin olive oil for drizzling

Instructions:

Prepare the Pizza Dough:

> In a bowl, combine warm water, sugar, and active dry yeast. Let it sit for about 5 minutes until it becomes frothy.

In a large mixing bowl, combine all-purpose flour and salt. Make a well in the center and pour in the yeast mixture and olive oil.

Mix until a dough forms, then knead on a floured surface for about 8-10 minutes until smooth.

Place the dough in a lightly oiled bowl, cover with a damp cloth, and let it rise in a warm place for about 1.5 to 2 hours, or until it doubles in size.

Prepare the Bolognese Sauce:

In a large skillet, brown the ground beef over medium-high heat. Drain excess fat if needed.

Add diced onion, carrot, and celery to the skillet. Sauté until the vegetables are softened.

Add minced garlic and continue to cook for another minute.

Pour in the tomato sauce and red wine (if using). Stir well.

Season with dried oregano, dried basil, salt, and black pepper. Simmer for about 20-30 minutes until the sauce thickens.

Assemble and Bake:

Preheat your oven to 475°F (245°C). If you have a pizza stone, place it in the oven while preheating.

Roll out the risen dough on a floured surface to your desired thickness.

Transfer the rolled-out dough to a pizza peel or parchment paper if using a baking sheet.

Spread the prepared Bolognese sauce evenly over the dough, leaving a small border around the edges.

Sprinkle shredded mozzarella cheese over the sauce.

Distribute grated Parmesan cheese evenly over the pizza.

If desired, sprinkle red pepper flakes for a hint of heat.

If using a pizza stone, carefully transfer the pizza to the preheated stone in the oven. If using a baking sheet, place it directly in the oven.

Bake for about 12-15 minutes or until the crust is golden and the cheese is melted.

Once out of the oven, let it cool for a minute, then garnish with fresh basil leaves and drizzle with extra-virgin olive oil.

Slice and savor the deliciousness of Bolognese Pizza!

Feel free to add additional toppings like olives or mushrooms to suit your taste. Buon appetito!

BBQ Chicken Pizza

Ingredients:

For the Pizza Dough:

- 4 cups all-purpose flour
- 2 teaspoons active dry yeast
- 1 1/2 cups warm water
- 2 tablespoons olive oil
- 1 teaspoon sugar
- 1 teaspoon salt

For the BBQ Chicken Topping:

- 1 cup cooked and shredded chicken breast
- 1/2 cup barbecue sauce (choose your favorite)
- 1/2 red onion, thinly sliced
- 1 cup shredded mozzarella cheese
- 1/2 cup cheddar cheese, shredded
- Fresh cilantro, chopped (for garnish)
- Red pepper flakes (optional)
- Cornmeal or flour (for dusting)

Instructions:

Prepare the Pizza Dough:

In a bowl, combine warm water, sugar, and active dry yeast. Let it sit for about 5 minutes until it becomes frothy.
In a large mixing bowl, combine all-purpose flour and salt. Make a well in the center and pour in the yeast mixture and olive oil.
Mix until a dough forms, then knead on a floured surface for about 8-10 minutes until smooth.
Place the dough in a lightly oiled bowl, cover with a damp cloth, and let it rise in a warm place for about 1.5 to 2 hours, or until it doubles in size.

Prepare the BBQ Chicken Topping:

In a bowl, combine the shredded chicken with barbecue sauce, ensuring the chicken is well coated.

Assemble and Bake:

Preheat your oven to 475°F (245°C). If you have a pizza stone, place it in the oven while preheating.
Roll out the risen dough on a floured surface to your desired thickness.
Transfer the rolled-out dough to a pizza peel or parchment paper if using a baking sheet, dusted with cornmeal or flour.
Spread the barbecue sauce-coated shredded chicken evenly over the dough.
Sprinkle sliced red onions, shredded mozzarella, and cheddar cheese over the chicken.
If desired, add a sprinkle of red pepper flakes for some heat.
If using a pizza stone, carefully transfer the pizza to the preheated stone in the oven. If using a baking sheet, place it directly in the oven.
Bake for about 12-15 minutes or until the crust is golden and the cheese is melted and bubbly.
Once out of the oven, sprinkle chopped fresh cilantro over the top.
Allow the pizza to cool for a minute, then slice and serve.
Enjoy the deliciousness of homemade BBQ Chicken Pizza!

Feel free to customize by adding other toppings like sliced bell peppers or jalapeños according to your preferences. Buon appetito!

Gourmet and Unique Pizzas:

Fig and Prosciutto Pizza

Ingredients:

For the Pizza Dough:

- 4 cups all-purpose flour
- 2 teaspoons active dry yeast
- 1 1/2 cups warm water
- 2 tablespoons olive oil
- 1 teaspoon sugar
- 1 teaspoon salt

For the Pizza Toppings:

- 1/2 cup fig jam or fresh figs, sliced
- 6-8 slices of prosciutto
- 1 cup fresh mozzarella cheese, torn into pieces
- 1/4 cup goat cheese, crumbled
- 1/4 cup balsamic glaze
- Fresh arugula (for topping)
- Extra-virgin olive oil for drizzling
- Salt and black pepper to taste

Instructions:

Prepare the Pizza Dough:

In a bowl, combine warm water, sugar, and active dry yeast. Let it sit for about 5 minutes until it becomes frothy.
In a large mixing bowl, combine all-purpose flour and salt. Make a well in the center and pour in the yeast mixture and olive oil.
Mix until a dough forms, then knead on a floured surface for about 8-10 minutes until smooth.
Place the dough in a lightly oiled bowl, cover with a damp cloth, and let it rise in a warm place for about 1.5 to 2 hours, or until it doubles in size.

Assemble and Bake:

Preheat your oven to 475°F (245°C). If you have a pizza stone, place it in the oven while preheating.

Roll out the risen dough on a floured surface to your desired thickness.

Transfer the rolled-out dough to a pizza peel or parchment paper if using a baking sheet.

Spread fig jam evenly over the dough or arrange fresh fig slices.

Tear pieces of fresh mozzarella and distribute them over the figs.

Place slices of prosciutto over the pizza.

Crumble goat cheese over the top.

Season with salt and black pepper to taste.

If using a pizza stone, carefully transfer the pizza to the preheated stone in the oven. If using a baking sheet, place it directly in the oven.

Bake for about 12-15 minutes or until the crust is golden, the cheese is melted, and the prosciutto becomes slightly crispy.

Once out of the oven, drizzle balsamic glaze over the pizza.

Top with fresh arugula and drizzle with extra-virgin olive oil.

Allow the pizza to cool for a minute, then slice and serve.

Enjoy the gourmet and unique flavors of Fig and Prosciutto Pizza!

Feel free to add a sprinkle of crushed red pepper for a hint of heat or experiment with different types of cheese to suit your taste. Buon appetito!

Smoked Salmon Pizza

Ingredients:

For the Pizza Dough:

- 4 cups all-purpose flour
- 2 teaspoons active dry yeast
- 1 1/2 cups warm water
- 2 tablespoons olive oil
- 1 teaspoon sugar
- 1 teaspoon salt

For the Pizza Toppings:

- 1/2 cup crème fraîche or cream cheese
- 1 tablespoon lemon juice
- 1 teaspoon lemon zest
- 8-10 slices smoked salmon
- 1/4 red onion, thinly sliced
- Capers, to taste
- Fresh dill, chopped, for garnish
- Freshly ground black pepper, to taste
- Arugula (optional, for topping after baking)
- Extra-virgin olive oil for drizzling

Instructions:

Prepare the Pizza Dough:

> In a bowl, combine warm water, sugar, and active dry yeast. Let it sit for about 5 minutes until it becomes frothy.
> In a large mixing bowl, combine all-purpose flour and salt. Make a well in the center and pour in the yeast mixture and olive oil.
> Mix until a dough forms, then knead on a floured surface for about 8-10 minutes until smooth.
> Place the dough in a lightly oiled bowl, cover with a damp cloth, and let it rise in a warm place for about 1.5 to 2 hours, or until it doubles in size.

Assemble and Bake:

Preheat your oven to 475°F (245°C). If you have a pizza stone, place it in the oven while preheating.

Roll out the risen dough on a floured surface to your desired thickness.

Transfer the rolled-out dough to a pizza peel or parchment paper if using a baking sheet.

In a small bowl, mix crème fraîche or cream cheese with lemon juice and lemon zest.

Spread the crème fraîche mixture evenly over the pizza dough, leaving a small border around the edges.

Arrange slices of smoked salmon on top of the crème fraîche.

Scatter thinly sliced red onion and capers over the salmon.

Grind black pepper over the pizza to taste.

If using a pizza stone, carefully transfer the pizza to the preheated stone in the oven. If using a baking sheet, place it directly in the oven.

Bake for about 12-15 minutes or until the crust is golden and the edges are crispy.

Once out of the oven, sprinkle chopped fresh dill over the pizza.

Optionally, top with fresh arugula for a peppery kick.

Drizzle with extra-virgin olive oil.

Allow the pizza to cool for a minute, then slice and serve.

Enjoy the elegant and delicious flavors of Smoked Salmon Pizza!

Feel free to customize by adding a squeeze of fresh lemon juice or experimenting with different toppings like sliced avocado or cherry tomatoes. Buon appetito!

Pumpkin and Sage Pizza

Ingredients:

For the Pizza Dough:

- 4 cups all-purpose flour
- 2 teaspoons active dry yeast
- 1 1/2 cups warm water
- 2 tablespoons olive oil
- 1 teaspoon sugar
- 1 teaspoon salt

For the Pumpkin Sauce:

- 1 cup pumpkin puree (canned or homemade)
- 2 cloves garlic, minced
- 1/2 teaspoon ground nutmeg
- Salt and black pepper to taste

For the Pizza Toppings:

- 1 1/2 cups shredded mozzarella cheese
- 1/2 cup crumbled goat cheese
- Fresh sage leaves
- 1/4 cup toasted pine nuts
- 1/4 cup grated Parmesan cheese
- Red pepper flakes (optional)
- Extra-virgin olive oil for drizzling

Instructions:

Prepare the Pizza Dough:

In a bowl, combine warm water, sugar, and active dry yeast. Let it sit for about 5 minutes until it becomes frothy.

In a large mixing bowl, combine all-purpose flour and salt. Make a well in the center and pour in the yeast mixture and olive oil.

Mix until a dough forms, then knead on a floured surface for about 8-10 minutes until smooth.

Place the dough in a lightly oiled bowl, cover with a damp cloth, and let it rise in a warm place for about 1.5 to 2 hours, or until it doubles in size.

Prepare the Pumpkin Sauce:

In a small saucepan, combine pumpkin puree, minced garlic, ground nutmeg, salt, and black pepper.
Heat over medium-low heat, stirring frequently, until the sauce is warmed through. Set aside.

Assemble and Bake:

Preheat your oven to 475°F (245°C). If you have a pizza stone, place it in the oven while preheating.
Roll out the risen dough on a floured surface to your desired thickness.
Transfer the rolled-out dough to a pizza peel or parchment paper if using a baking sheet.
Spread the pumpkin sauce evenly over the pizza dough, leaving a small border around the edges.
Sprinkle shredded mozzarella cheese over the pumpkin sauce.
Crumble goat cheese over the pizza.
Distribute fresh sage leaves evenly on top.
Sprinkle toasted pine nuts and grated Parmesan cheese over the pizza.
If desired, add red pepper flakes for a hint of heat.
If using a pizza stone, carefully transfer the pizza to the preheated stone in the oven. If using a baking sheet, place it directly in the oven.
Bake for about 12-15 minutes or until the crust is golden and the cheese is melted.
Once out of the oven, drizzle with extra-virgin olive oil.
Allow the pizza to cool for a minute, then slice and serve.
Enjoy the delightful and seasonal flavors of Pumpkin and Sage Pizza!

Feel free to customize by adding caramelized onions or a balsamic glaze drizzle for extra depth of flavor. Buon appetito!

Caprese Salad Pizza

Ingredients:

For the Pizza Dough:

- 4 cups all-purpose flour
- 2 teaspoons active dry yeast
- 1 1/2 cups warm water
- 2 tablespoons olive oil
- 1 teaspoon sugar
- 1 teaspoon salt

For the Pizza Sauce:

- 1 cup cherry tomatoes, halved
- 1 cup fresh mozzarella cheese, sliced or torn into pieces
- Fresh basil leaves, torn
- 2 tablespoons balsamic glaze
- Extra-virgin olive oil for drizzling
- Salt and black pepper to taste

Instructions:

Prepare the Pizza Dough:

In a bowl, combine warm water, sugar, and active dry yeast. Let it sit for about 5 minutes until it becomes frothy.
In a large mixing bowl, combine all-purpose flour and salt. Make a well in the center and pour in the yeast mixture and olive oil.
Mix until a dough forms, then knead on a floured surface for about 8-10 minutes until smooth.
Place the dough in a lightly oiled bowl, cover with a damp cloth, and let it rise in a warm place for about 1.5 to 2 hours, or until it doubles in size.

Assemble and Bake:

Preheat your oven to 475°F (245°C). If you have a pizza stone, place it in the oven while preheating.
Roll out the risen dough on a floured surface to your desired thickness.

Transfer the rolled-out dough to a pizza peel or parchment paper if using a baking sheet.
Arrange halved cherry tomatoes and fresh mozzarella pieces evenly over the pizza dough.
Season with salt and black pepper to taste.
If using a pizza stone, carefully transfer the pizza to the preheated stone in the oven. If using a baking sheet, place it directly in the oven.
Bake for about 12-15 minutes or until the crust is golden and the cheese is melted and bubbly.
Once out of the oven, sprinkle torn fresh basil leaves over the pizza.
Drizzle balsamic glaze and extra-virgin olive oil over the top.
Allow the pizza to cool for a minute, then slice and serve.
Enjoy the light and refreshing flavors of Caprese Salad Pizza!

Feel free to add a sprinkle of red pepper flakes for a hint of heat or experiment with other ingredients like arugula or a drizzle of pesto. Buon appetito!

Dessert Pizzas:

Nutella and Strawberry Dessert Pizza

Ingredients:

For the Pizza Dough:

- 4 cups all-purpose flour
- 2 teaspoons active dry yeast
- 1 1/2 cups warm water
- 2 tablespoons olive oil
- 1 teaspoon sugar
- 1 teaspoon salt

For the Dessert Toppings:

- Nutella (as needed)
- Fresh strawberries, sliced
- Sliced bananas (optional)
- Chopped hazelnuts or almonds (optional)
- Powdered sugar (for dusting)
- Mint leaves (for garnish, optional)

Instructions:

Prepare the Pizza Dough:

> In a bowl, combine warm water, sugar, and active dry yeast. Let it sit for about 5 minutes until it becomes frothy.
> In a large mixing bowl, combine all-purpose flour and salt. Make a well in the center and pour in the yeast mixture and olive oil.
> Mix until a dough forms, then knead on a floured surface for about 8-10 minutes until smooth.
> Place the dough in a lightly oiled bowl, cover with a damp cloth, and let it rise in a warm place for about 1.5 to 2 hours, or until it doubles in size.

Assemble and Bake:

Preheat your oven to 475°F (245°C). If you have a pizza stone, place it in the oven while preheating.

Roll out the risen dough on a floured surface to your desired thickness.

Transfer the rolled-out dough to a pizza peel or parchment paper if using a baking sheet.

Bake the pizza crust for about 8-10 minutes or until it's just starting to turn golden. This ensures the crust is cooked through but not overly browned.

Allow the crust to cool slightly.

Spread a generous layer of Nutella over the partially cooled pizza crust.

Arrange sliced strawberries (and sliced bananas, if using) over the Nutella.

If desired, sprinkle chopped hazelnuts or almonds over the top for added crunch.

Dust the entire pizza with powdered sugar.

Optionally, garnish with fresh mint leaves for a burst of freshness.

Slice the Nutella and Strawberry Dessert Pizza into wedges and serve.

Enjoy the indulgent and sweet flavors of this delightful dessert pizza!

Feel free to get creative with additional toppings like shredded coconut or a drizzle of caramel. It's a versatile dessert that you can customize to suit your taste. Buon appetito!

Cannoli Pizza

Ingredients:

For the Pizza Dough:

- 4 cups all-purpose flour
- 2 teaspoons active dry yeast
- 1 1/2 cups warm water
- 2 tablespoons olive oil
- 1 teaspoon sugar
- 1 teaspoon salt

For the Cannoli Topping:

- 1 cup ricotta cheese
- 1/2 cup powdered sugar
- 1 teaspoon vanilla extract
- 1/4 cup mini chocolate chips
- 1/4 cup chopped pistachios
- Zest of 1 orange
- Honey (for drizzling)

Instructions:

Prepare the Pizza Dough:

In a bowl, combine warm water, sugar, and active dry yeast. Let it sit for about 5 minutes until it becomes frothy.

In a large mixing bowl, combine all-purpose flour and salt. Make a well in the center and pour in the yeast mixture and olive oil.

Mix until a dough forms, then knead on a floured surface for about 8-10 minutes until smooth.

Place the dough in a lightly oiled bowl, cover with a damp cloth, and let it rise in a warm place for about 1.5 to 2 hours, or until it doubles in size.

Prepare the Cannoli Topping:

In a bowl, combine ricotta cheese, powdered sugar, and vanilla extract. Mix until well combined.

Fold in mini chocolate chips, chopped pistachios, and orange zest into the ricotta mixture.

Assemble and Bake:

Preheat your oven to 475°F (245°C). If you have a pizza stone, place it in the oven while preheating.
Roll out the risen dough on a floured surface to your desired thickness.
Transfer the rolled-out dough to a pizza peel or parchment paper if using a baking sheet.
Spread the cannoli topping evenly over the pizza dough, leaving a small border around the edges.
If using a pizza stone, carefully transfer the pizza to the preheated stone in the oven. If using a baking sheet, place it directly in the oven.
Bake for about 12-15 minutes or until the crust is golden and the cannoli topping is set.
Once out of the oven, drizzle honey over the Cannoli Pizza.
Allow the pizza to cool for a minute, then slice and serve.
Enjoy the delightful combination of Cannoli flavors in pizza form!

This unique dessert pizza captures the essence of cannoli with its creamy ricotta, chocolate, and pistachio goodness. Feel free to experiment with additional toppings or variations to suit your taste. Buon appetito!

Tiramisu Pizza

Ingredients:

For the Pizza Dough:

- 4 cups all-purpose flour
- 2 teaspoons active dry yeast
- 1 1/2 cups warm water
- 2 tablespoons olive oil
- 1 teaspoon sugar
- 1 teaspoon salt

For the Tiramisu Topping:

- 1 cup mascarpone cheese
- 1/2 cup heavy cream
- 1/2 cup powdered sugar
- 1 teaspoon vanilla extract
- 1 cup strong brewed coffee, cooled
- 2 tablespoons coffee liqueur (optional)
- Cocoa powder, for dusting
- Chocolate shavings or grated chocolate, for garnish
- Ladyfinger cookies, for serving

Instructions:

Prepare the Pizza Dough:

> In a bowl, combine warm water, sugar, and active dry yeast. Let it sit for about 5 minutes until it becomes frothy.
> In a large mixing bowl, combine all-purpose flour and salt. Make a well in the center and pour in the yeast mixture and olive oil.
> Mix until a dough forms, then knead on a floured surface for about 8-10 minutes until smooth.
> Place the dough in a lightly oiled bowl, cover with a damp cloth, and let it rise in a warm place for about 1.5 to 2 hours, or until it doubles in size.

Prepare the Tiramisu Topping:

> In a bowl, whip the mascarpone cheese until smooth.

In a separate bowl, whip the heavy cream until stiff peaks form.
Gently fold the whipped cream into the mascarpone cheese.
Add powdered sugar and vanilla extract, and continue to fold until well combined.

Assemble and Serve:

Preheat your oven to 475°F (245°C). If you have a pizza stone, place it in the oven while preheating.
Roll out the risen dough on a floured surface to your desired thickness.
Transfer the rolled-out dough to a pizza peel or parchment paper if using a baking sheet.
Bake the pizza crust for about 8-10 minutes or until it's just starting to turn golden. This ensures the crust is cooked through but not overly browned.
Allow the crust to cool slightly.
Combine brewed coffee and coffee liqueur (if using) in a shallow dish.
Brush the coffee mixture over the partially cooled pizza crust.
Spread the Tiramisu topping evenly over the pizza crust.
Dust the entire pizza with cocoa powder.
Garnish with chocolate shavings or grated chocolate.
Serve the Tiramisu Pizza with ladyfinger cookies on the side.
Enjoy this unique and delicious dessert pizza!

Tiramisu Pizza brings together the iconic flavors of Tiramisu in a fun and shareable form. It's a delightful treat for any occasion. Buon appetito!

Apple Cinnamon Dessert Pizza

Ingredients:

For the Pizza Dough:

- 4 cups all-purpose flour
- 2 teaspoons active dry yeast
- 1 1/2 cups warm water
- 2 tablespoons olive oil
- 1 teaspoon sugar
- 1 teaspoon salt

For the Apple Topping:

- 3-4 medium-sized apples, peeled, cored, and thinly sliced (use a mix of sweet and tart apples)
- 1/4 cup unsalted butter
- 1/3 cup brown sugar
- 1 teaspoon ground cinnamon
- 1/4 teaspoon ground nutmeg
- 1 tablespoon lemon juice

For the Cream Cheese Drizzle:

- 4 oz cream cheese, softened
- 1/2 cup powdered sugar
- 1/2 teaspoon vanilla extract
- 2-3 tablespoons milk (adjust for desired consistency)

Optional Toppings:

- Chopped nuts (such as walnuts or pecans)
- Caramel sauce

Instructions:

Prepare the Pizza Dough:

In a bowl, combine warm water, sugar, and active dry yeast. Let it sit for about 5 minutes until it becomes frothy.

In a large mixing bowl, combine all-purpose flour and salt. Make a well in the center and pour in the yeast mixture and olive oil.

Mix until a dough forms, then knead on a floured surface for about 8-10 minutes until smooth.

Place the dough in a lightly oiled bowl, cover with a damp cloth, and let it rise in a warm place for about 1.5 to 2 hours, or until it doubles in size.

Prepare the Apple Topping:

In a skillet over medium heat, melt the butter.

Add sliced apples, brown sugar, ground cinnamon, ground nutmeg, and lemon juice to the skillet.

Cook, stirring occasionally, until the apples are tender and the sugar has caramelized, about 8-10 minutes. Set aside to cool.

Prepare the Cream Cheese Drizzle:

In a bowl, beat together softened cream cheese, powdered sugar, and vanilla extract until smooth.

Gradually add milk, 1 tablespoon at a time, until you achieve a drizzling consistency. Set aside.

Assemble and Serve:

Preheat your oven to 475°F (245°C). If you have a pizza stone, place it in the oven while preheating.

Roll out the risen dough on a floured surface to your desired thickness.

Transfer the rolled-out dough to a pizza peel or parchment paper if using a baking sheet.

Spread the cooked apple topping evenly over the pizza dough.

If using a pizza stone, carefully transfer the pizza to the preheated stone in the oven. If using a baking sheet, place it directly in the oven.

Bake for about 12-15 minutes or until the crust is golden.

Once out of the oven, drizzle the cream cheese mixture over the apple-topped pizza.

Optionally, sprinkle chopped nuts over the pizza and drizzle with caramel sauce.

Allow the pizza to cool for a few minutes, then slice and serve.

Enjoy the warm and comforting flavors of Apple Cinnamon Dessert Pizza!

This dessert pizza is a crowd-pleaser, combining the classic fall flavors of apples and cinnamon in a deliciously unique way. Buon appetito!

Chocolate and Marshmallow Pizza

Ingredients:

For the Pizza Dough:

- 4 cups all-purpose flour
- 2 teaspoons active dry yeast
- 1 1/2 cups warm water
- 2 tablespoons olive oil
- 1 teaspoon sugar
- 1 teaspoon salt

For the Chocolate and Marshmallow Topping:

- 1 cup chocolate chips (semi-sweet or milk chocolate)
- 1 cup mini marshmallows
- 1/2 cup crushed graham crackers
- 2 tablespoons unsalted butter, melted

Optional Toppings:

- Sliced strawberries, banana, or other fruits
- Chopped nuts (such as almonds or walnuts)
- Drizzle of caramel or chocolate sauce

Instructions:

Prepare the Pizza Dough:

> In a bowl, combine warm water, sugar, and active dry yeast. Let it sit for about 5 minutes until it becomes frothy.
> In a large mixing bowl, combine all-purpose flour and salt. Make a well in the center and pour in the yeast mixture and olive oil.
> Mix until a dough forms, then knead on a floured surface for about 8-10 minutes until smooth.
> Place the dough in a lightly oiled bowl, cover with a damp cloth, and let it rise in a warm place for about 1.5 to 2 hours, or until it doubles in size.

Assemble and Bake:

1. Preheat your oven to 475°F (245°C). If you have a pizza stone, place it in the oven while preheating.
2. Roll out the risen dough on a floured surface to your desired thickness.
3. Transfer the rolled-out dough to a pizza peel or parchment paper if using a baking sheet.
4. Brush the melted butter over the pizza crust.
5. Sprinkle chocolate chips evenly over the crust.
6. Distribute mini marshmallows over the chocolate chips.
7. Add any optional toppings, such as sliced strawberries, banana, or chopped nuts.
8. If using a pizza stone, carefully transfer the pizza to the preheated stone in the oven. If using a baking sheet, place it directly in the oven.
9. Bake for about 10-12 minutes or until the crust is golden, and the chocolate and marshmallows are melted and gooey.
10. Once out of the oven, sprinkle crushed graham crackers over the pizza.
11. Optional: Drizzle with caramel or chocolate sauce for extra sweetness.
12. Allow the pizza to cool for a few minutes, then slice and serve.
13. Enjoy the gooey and chocolatey goodness of Chocolate and Marshmallow Pizza!

This dessert pizza is a fun and indulgent treat, perfect for sharing with friends and family. Feel free to get creative with additional toppings or variations. Buon appetito!

www.ingramcontent.com/pod-product-compliance
Lightning Source LLC
LaVergne TN
LVHW081318060526
838201LV00055B/2352